AF480973

Trap Poems

&

Lit Drawings

David Aaron Greenberg

with an introduction by
Oliver Tompkins Ray

Cover Image *Trio* by David Aaron Greenberg
Author Image by Barron Claiborne
Design by Matt Lacognata
Edited by Nora Tofigh

ISBN: 979-8-218-30599-4
First Edition

Published by: Trops Publishing
tropspublishing.com
New York, NY

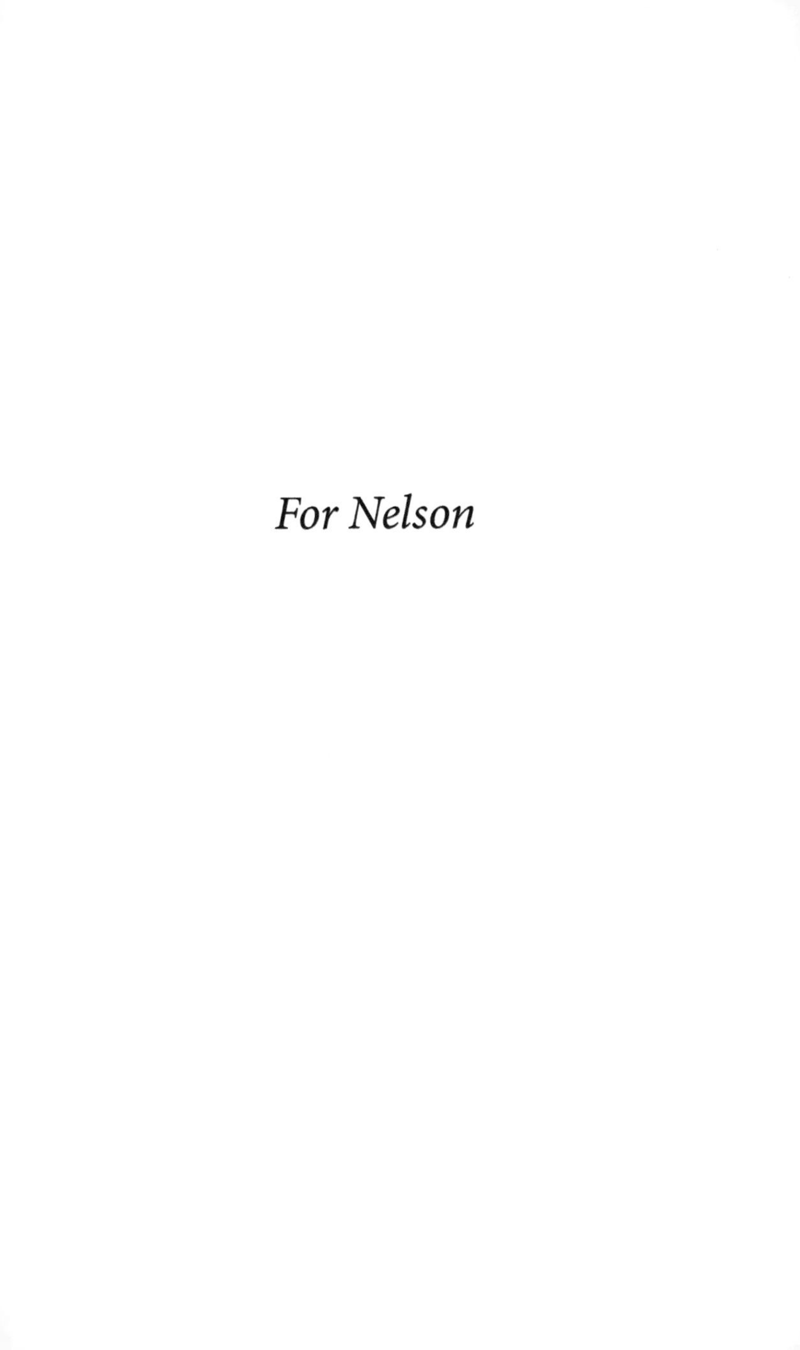

For Nelson

*Take a look at a poem.
Read a drawing or two.
This book is open for you
to browse, carouse with, drift
into and out from, study,
criticize, vibe with or
to be amused, bemused,
inspired by or simply satisfied.*

*Some of these poems
I've read before crowds,
some I've whispered
to myself alone.*

*Most of these drawings were
made from life directly—
a few came to me in the space
between a memory and a dream.*

CONTENTS

Trap Poems

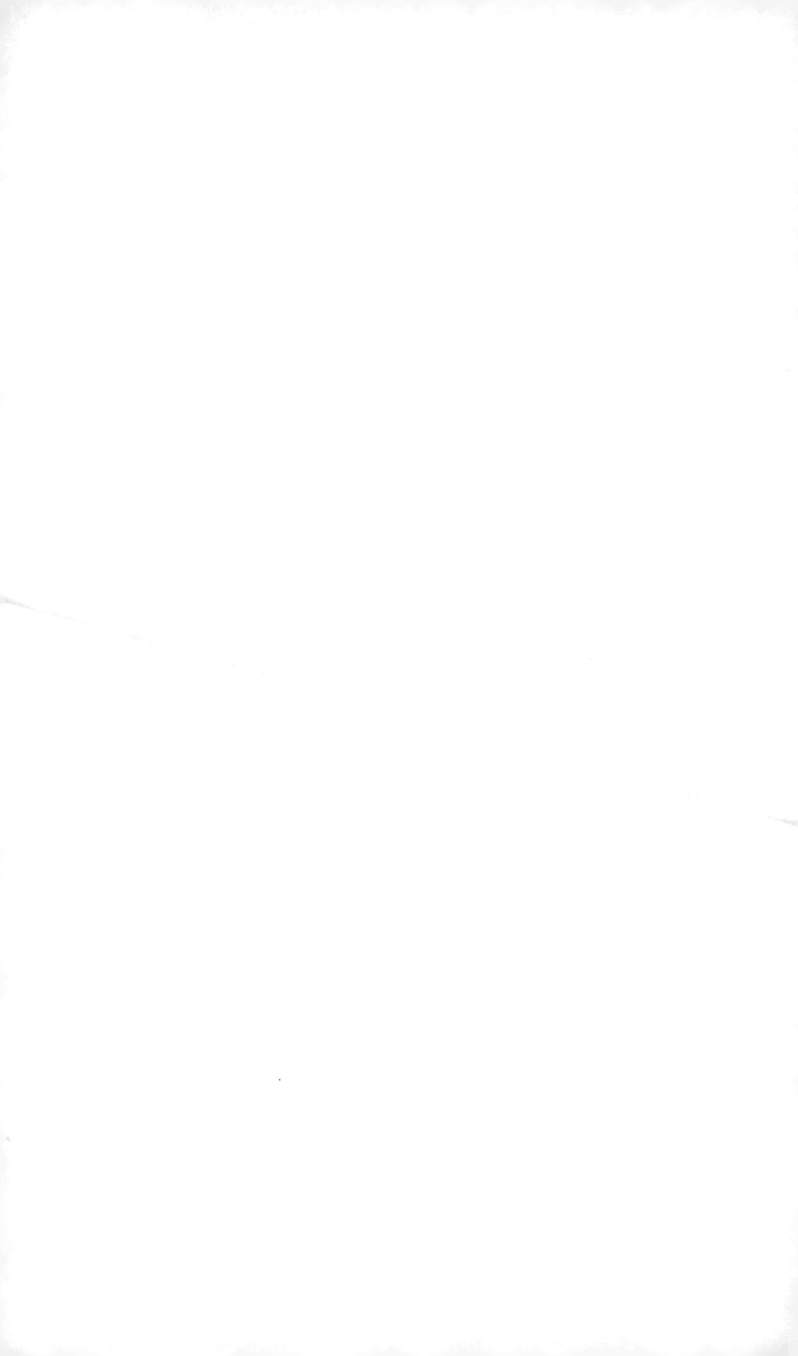

Introduction

Imagine boy Greenberg listening to early 80's Tri-state area pop radio— all the hooks, he swallows them whole, absorbs them with his soul until they become part of his DNA: Grand Master Flash, Madonna, UTFO, the Police, U2 merging into the Smiths, the Cure. While the center of the United States is eating Twinkies and dealing with the issues of *Footloose*, boy Greenberg is osmosing the rainbow lights of Manhattan, pink triangles, Silence = Death stencils. He has a crush on a cute girl in his class. He notices how beautiful the skin of the boy across from him on the school bus is. He's smart. He sees how things work, like one of those kids that can take apart a motor and put it back together— in Greenberg's case the motors are hearts, what makes them beat, harder. His mother loves him. He does well in school. He discovers poetry.

Suddenly all the pop hooks start merging with the lyric line— poetry sings in him and he can't tell anymore whether it's Morrissey or Keats. It doesn't matter. The call heard long ago becomes a melody. He picks up a guitar, he strums a chord. The chord shakes the ground, so he strums another; again the ground shakes and he strums a third— he's written his first song. Walt Whitman's ghost is swimming beneath the George Washington Bridge. From the bus window Greenberg can see every drop of the Hudson River glisten on Walt's skin; the books on his lap give him a hard-on. Where's he going? He's going to buy some records in the Village and those records are books. The radio is a library; the library is a disco. He goes to college. He does well. He is the top of his class.

Then one day an old poet comes to town. Greenberg has
a mother. He's looking for a father now. A father, a man,
someone who can, as he kneels before him, rest a sword, first
on one shoulder, then the other, and tell him he's a knight;
He's been admitted in to the backroom of the greatest club of
all— the one that stands above Max's Kansas City or Studio
54— the club with a velvet rope made of light, it's called
Poetry. Beneath the eaves of St. Mark's Church, the creepy
statues as his witness, he walks beside the living masters,
eats potato pancakes at Veselka with a member of the true
royal family of England (every word of *Sandanista* written in
applesauce on his skull), is heckled with love by the baddest
boy of the Beats, the one with the biggest heart.

Are these poems? Are these songs? Does it make a difference? This is where it's at now, when the younger becomes
the elder, the student the teacher, the boy the man— this
is when the word becomes something you'll never be able
to spell because the dead have had their way with it and
because of that, the hands of the ancestors, it is holy.

                              Oliver Tompkins Ray

Good Evening

This is not my last temptation
Or a cause to be alarmed

I forgot my harmonica
But I still head out
Into the streets
To look for an honest face

I'm not going very far
And you're not that far behind

Anyone could be waiting for you
And you could be anything
Or everything
Except the rain

Happy Ending

A light bulb blows out
The phone doesn't ring
I've got my suspicions
And you have your fists

I'm feeling creepy
I'm feeling blessed
I want to kiss you

Regardless the risk

Darkness stretches
Across your cheek
An incomplete sentence
Or something obsolete

Let me begin again

A narrative
In first person
With the last chapter
Missing in action

Where did our happy ending go?
Where did our once upon a time lead?

To after hours bars
And new spots to cop
Empty parks
And public bathrooms

Times Square
Astor Place
Or those exotic stops

The bodega
At Third & C

It's the same old scene
Cigarettes and scary dreams
Midnight sidewalks
And eyes of green

I hear you whisper
When I scream
I feel you breathing
Next to me

A suitcase of memory

Get this picture down
White underwear
An empty glass

A door without a keyhole

I'm half a word away
And I'm not sorry

A shift in weight
That took a thousand years
To properly name
Contrapposto

Seen in Rome
On a Vespa
Or in New Jersey
On a skateboard

But no one's got
A good idea
To paint on a ceiling
Anymore

Moms Blue Calypso

Moms blue calypso
strum with rum
and the only one
I knew who could purr
in my ear like a cat
on a black top roof
inclined to be the best
one I'll ever find

Moms blue calypso
sublime and sharp
in the key of need
can play it on Saturday
but everyday
feels like Monday
when the weight
of the Ocean
drains your eyes
of light
and the heavy
lidded solemnity
ain't a'ight

don't lie to me now
don't lie to me son
don't cry for me child
just smile for me once

Moms blue calypso
plucked and picked
On a tranquilo guitar
willed to me by Gloria
G-L-O-R-I-A Gloria
capo'd on the first fret
and I bet you knew it
before I blew it
lips puckered

to los limones
para mi
para ti
para the party
in the Hotel Chelsea
when the moon
was creeping in
and the streets of Cairo
were filled with red banners
of a hapless sort of hope

Moms blue calypso
sung softly
to the motherless child
who sleeps in Antigua
while cops stand around
on Staten Island
and watch a giant collapse
in a heap of flesh
disinterested in life
those half zombies
and they walk around like
prison guards
'cos they know
we're all on death row

don't lie to me now
don't lie to me son
don't cry for me child
just smile for me once

Lack Like

All you selfish pricks
With your selfie clicks
And your likes and likes
Without even a thought
To enlist or even
Evolve past your
Self-interest or
Even dislike or
Discuss the currency
Of your lust
Nor the dust that's settled
On your real life
So uptight but so
Loose and lovely
In the light from the screen

I scream into micro-
phones but no one
listens

I tap and prod
And I peek and poke
But the letters like spokes
In a wheel are broke
And ain't nobody no-
body gonna fix 'em
when you're a nobody
no body—

and the elixir to this
mix is I know I
do it all too—I am
become death
destroyer of illusions
utilized to replace
my delusions which
have dissipated over

the years spent
guarded from the
bombardment of images
barreling towards me
like headlights on the
New Jersey Turnpike
And there are times
when I do feel connected
to the power source
when deliberate accidents
happen and I use
the illusions to manifest
real life
spirit clicks

More than toe
jobs or ankle licks—
a desperate yearning
for the ultimate sex
Drugs and money

Chill

Close the door
sit down
and chill

There's silence
to fill
if you want me to
I will

Or you can
stand inside the rain
and watch it wash away
all those yesterdays

Talk to me
It shouldn't
have to be
such a mystery

I've been running around
this town

chasing after
this and that

Falling in
and fading out

Close the door
sit down
and chill

I want to hear
every chapter
of your story

Damian

Hell yeah
He blurts out
with equal parts
guttural gumption
and sly sophistication

He knows
he's got to
keep the dive bar rocking

and never give up
the game

Then there are
those stolen moments—
sublime for their infrequency
as much as their utter charm—
when the puckish grin subsides
and he downshifts
to a gentle roar

That's when you can hear
the almost wounded heart
pound out its primordial beat

And I can't help but to sigh
for all the useless rain

that penetrates the Atlantic's
surface—all that slick wood
that glistens on the boardwalk
where he once stood

armed with a smile
and a thousand
miles yet to be seen

Inside Your Song

The fear of
making it up
as I go along
just to make it
through
a gallery
of tears

It keeps us
questioning
agendas

At some point

I let my
imagination
open up
your door

B.C.

I can't
blush
I'm black
he said

and loaded
up his pipe

take what

he proclaims
as gospel
at your own
chosen speed

his instincts
are always
precise

whether
strong
or wrong

and
ever since he
sold his crown

he's free
to make
majestic
from light
and skin

that which
most kings
could never
imagine

Snap Shot

I can't talk my way
Out of this picture
The light's all wrong
Only shadows in negative space
I can't quite make out

The face
But I know
It's there

The opposite of everything is love

I love you
It's all I can do

I can't fight my way
Out of this plastic bag
From fire to ash
To blister
I put your cigarette out
Before the afterglow
On my arm

I never quit smoking
Because I never started

I was just thinking
About you
It's never the right thing to do
I borrowed your best excuse
Some magic dust
An incantation
And poof
You disappeared
Into the pollution
Of the moment

I never bought you flowers
But I ripped some out
Of the ground
Outside your apartment
And stuck them
In a glass
It all gets a little fuzzy
I think I fell asleep

The opposite of everything is love

Me And Your Shadow

The music falls on deaf ears
For years I remained
As in an elevator going up

I should kiss your feet
Wash your toes
With my tongue
Dry them with my hair

But I won't
At least not now
Not here

Fortune makes fools
When the morning comes
In the final judgment
I finally gave up

I can say nothing new
About death
Out of my head
Gone gone gone

Just when you think
You have seen it all
Someone shows you more

Down on all fours
Ready to adore
Painted nails
Black Jack hands
Little spikes in their hair

It's not me on horseback
I simply wanted to hear
Your breath in my ear

A simple song
To long for a home

The sooner you rise
The sooner you fall in love

The sooner you try
The sooner you know

It's too deep to feel shallow
It's just me and your shadow

Lounging under the moon
If you should mean
So much to us
Or to me

Forget the movie
Just listen
To the soundtrack

She Got The Silver

She developed
a taste
for fine things
and eventually
expected others
to pay for them

She lived off her
occasional charm
and reluctant wit
believing herself
above the muck
she created

Trafficking in
gypsy daydreams
empty palmistry
wounded witchcraft
and a genuine touch
with the brush

In a flash
she could be
as gentle
as a rash
or subtle
like a fist of cash

She'd offer you
a bowl of borscht
expecting nothing
more than a hearty
appetite

and maybe
a new spoon
depending
on the quality
of your mercy

and of course
the silver

The Village

There was a dream
that was the City

Our work was
worthless
Because it was
priceless

At least
To us

What difference
does it make
The truth about you
and me

And the whole
Scene

I look back fondly
And rejoice
in the present
eternally

Tight or taboo
You're still a boo

In someone's
Eyes

Preambling is not
Rambling or ambling

Get to the point

Don't explain
your explanations

Don't bore us
Get to the chorus

Love is that feeling you get
Right before you vomit

That was something
you wrote one night
On a stretched canvas

I knew what you meant
It was elegant

Even as high
As you were

You still had a natural
Ability to construct

A great piece

The problem was always
The drugs didn't work
They made it worse
And of course
They killed you

Preambling isn't rambling
Or dangling the sordid detail

Eventually
You do get
To the point

Streets

The stellar gray
urban decay

This is all to say
That I'm alive today

The haze that fades
The radio waves

I'm back in my car
heading out to play
In the snaps
culled from heavenly
patches of sunlight
pot smoke
last night's red light
lapsed memory
mementos

a hip hop beat
a pause in the steam
the Puerto Rican girl's
breath breaks in waves
against the bodega
wall gently

this is all to say
that I'm alive today
still searching
for that sympathetic fix

a face half-formed
in the twilight

still searching
for that perfect
picture

Swathed in sexy
sadness
or was that
madness

I'm glad at last
for a hint

of soulful eyes
distracted and sublime
I stay high all the time

A hit and a slant rhyme
most times

Refined behind a line
I am what I am after hours
Divine

this is all to say
that I'm alive today
still searching
for that sympathetic fix

The stellar gray
urban decay
The haze that fades
The radio waves

This is all to say
that I'm alive today

I'm alive

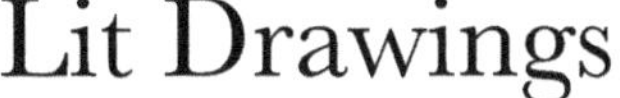

Lit Drawings

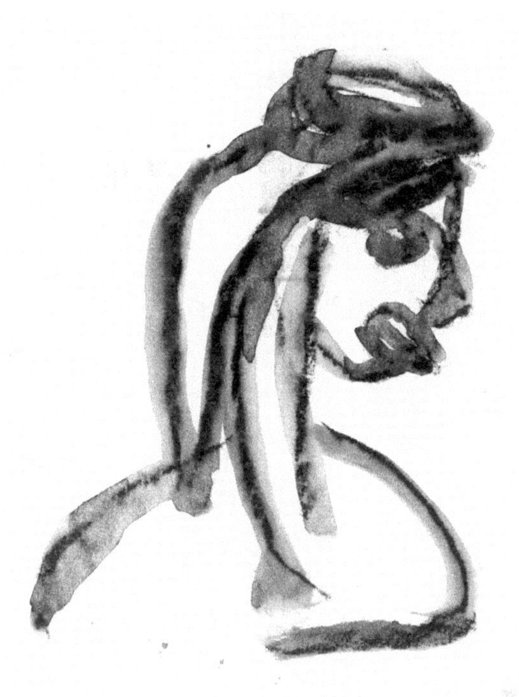

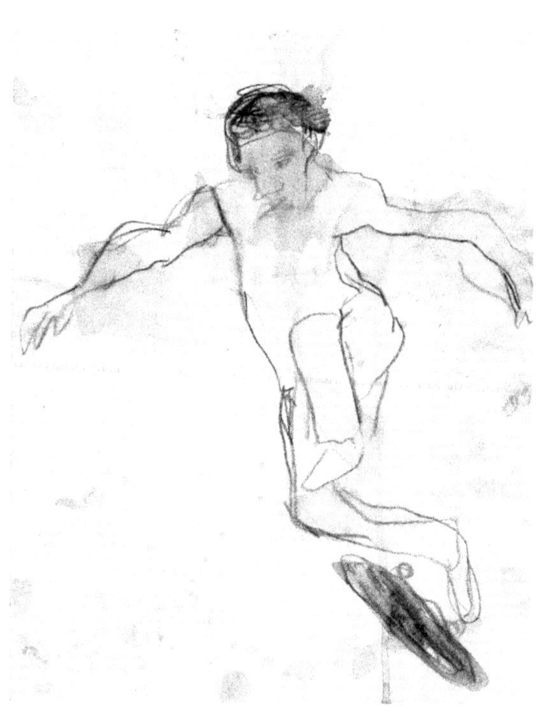

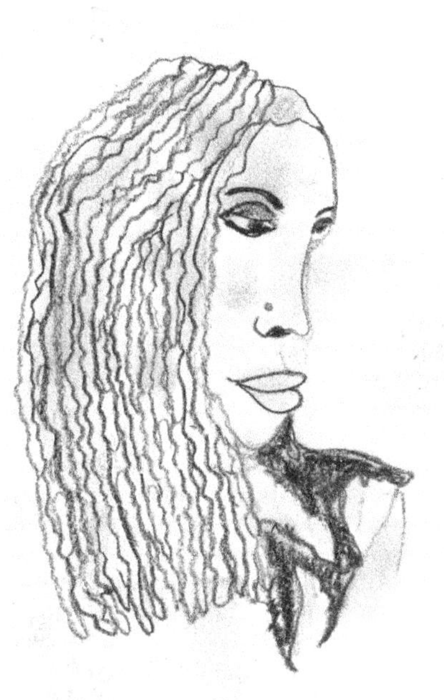

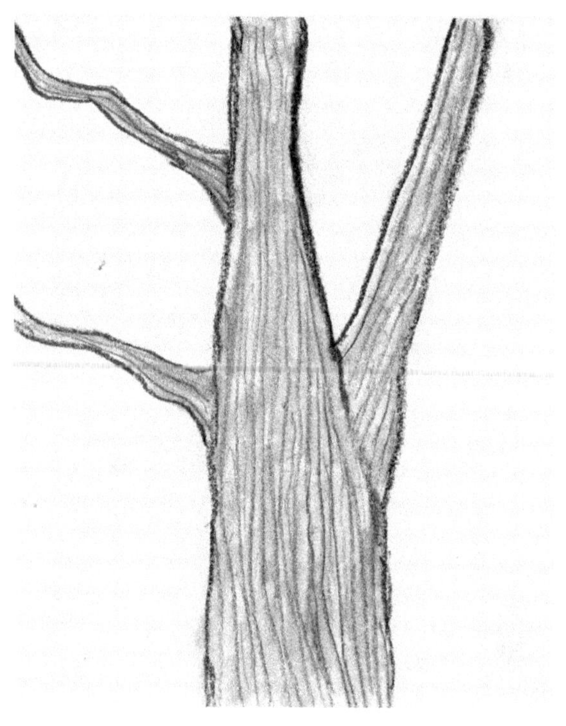

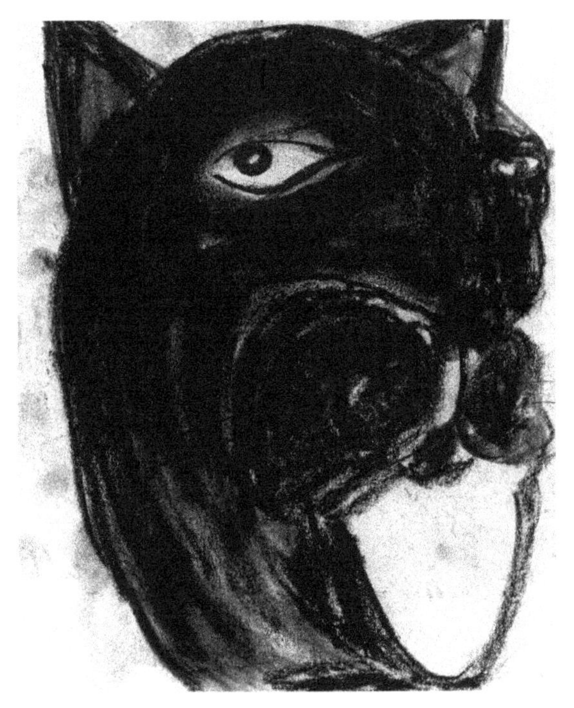

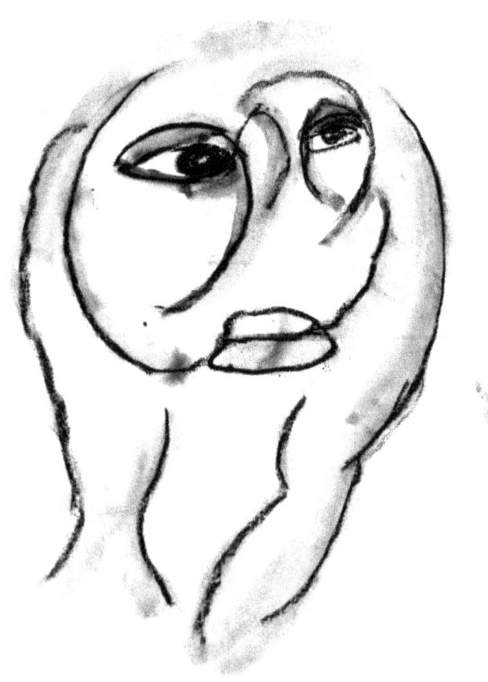

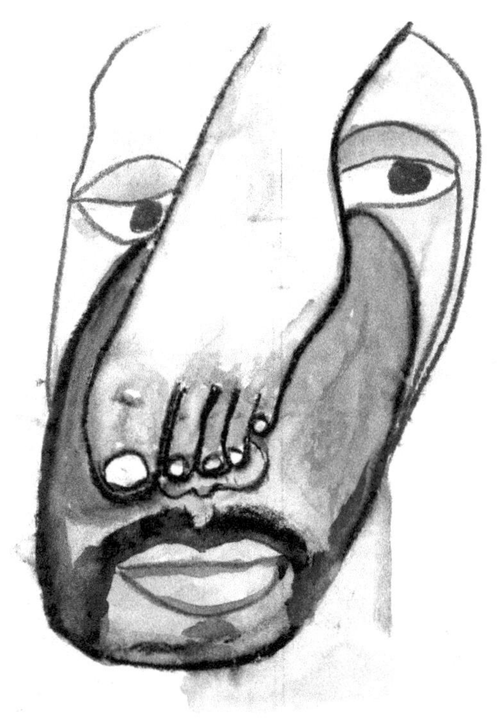

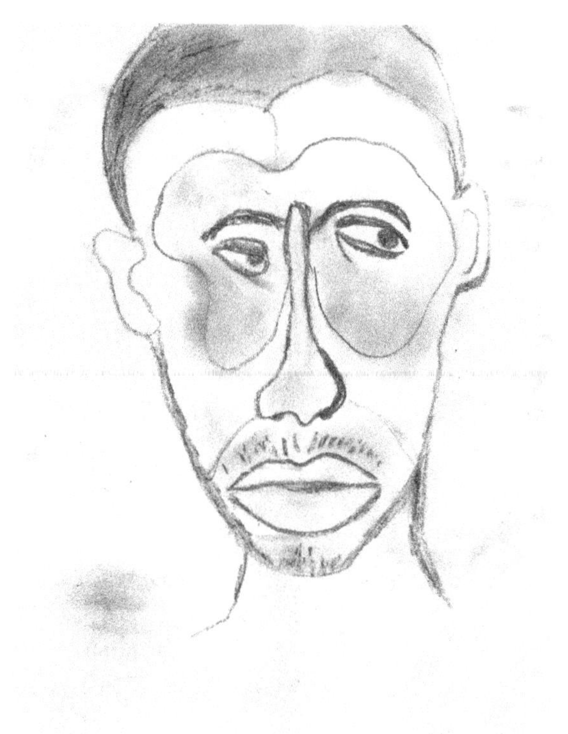

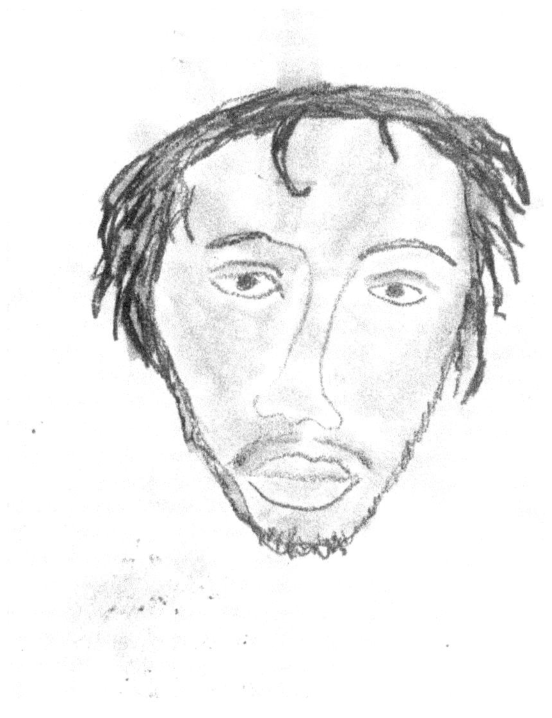

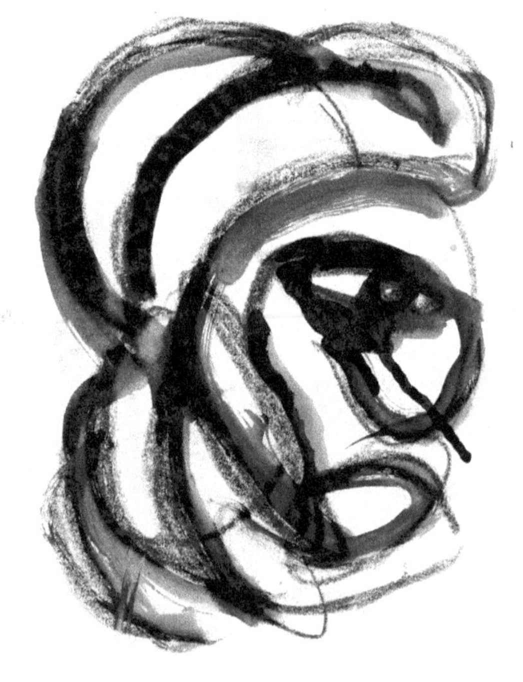

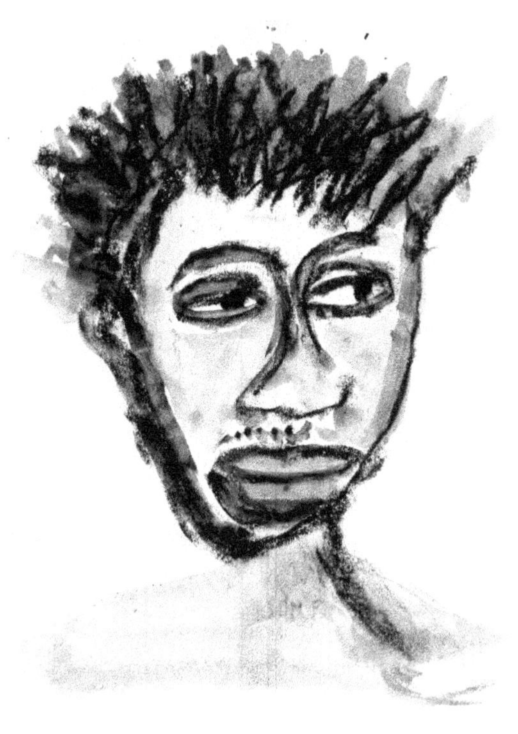

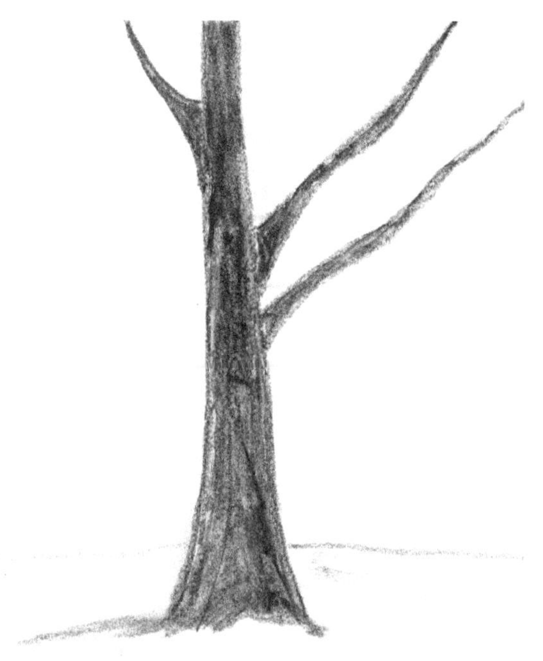

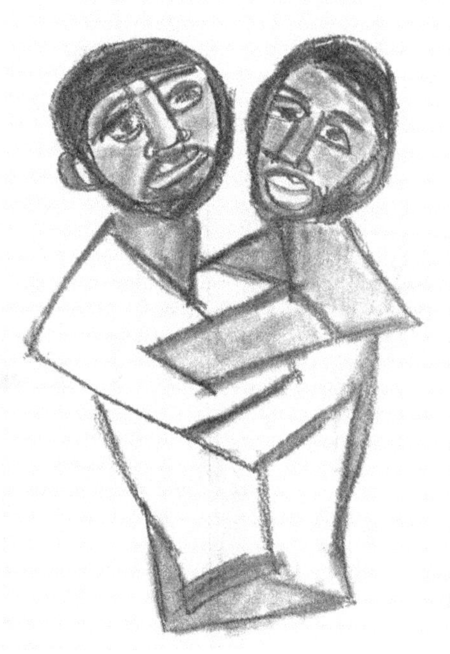

Index

Acknowledgements

Special thanks to Nora Tofigh for her tireless efforts in the creation of this book.

Thank you David Sisko, Evan Williamson, Sandflower Dyson, Oliver Tompkins Ray, Barron Claiborne, Nemo Librizzi, John Matthews, Daniel Wolfskehl, Hans Viets, Darren Bader, Gregory Schwartz, Damian Rucci and Cord Moreski.

In loving memory of Carol N Greenberg 1945-2023